MW00512844

iO

RESEARCH REPORT SEPTEMBER 2013

Teacher Evaluation in Practice
Implementing Chicago's REACH Students

Susan E. Sporte, W. David Stevens, Kaleen Healey, Jennie Jiang, and Holly Hart

TABLE OF CONTENTS

Acknowledgements

The authors gratefully acknowledge the support of the Joyce Foundation and its continuing interest in this important line of work. This analysis based on one district's experience with a dramatically different teacher evaluation system could not have happened without Joyce's steadfast support and long term commitment. In addition we would like to acknowledge the support of Chicago Public Schools and the Chicago Teachers Union. We have gained particular insights from Matt Lyons, Paulette Poncelet, Sheila Cashman, Elizabeth Press, Didi Schwartz, Amanda Smith, Susan Kajiwara-Ansai, and Meghan Zefran from CPS central office and from Carol Caref of the CTU as well as other teachers from the CPS-CTU Joint Committee who have provided valuable feedback as the work has progressed.

In addition we thank the teachers and administrators of Chicago Public Schools who shared their thoughts through multiple surveys, and those who provided their valuable time in one-on-one interviews. This report was made possible through their participation. We also learned from those individuals serving as Instructional Effectiveness Specialists and thank them for the extra time they spent sharing with us.

We are also indebted to the Research Assistants who helped in countless ways to make this report possible: Patrick Wu, Elc Estrera, Jen Cowhy, Catherine Alvarez-McCurdy, Josie Glore, and Gabrielle Friedman. Their contributions have been invaluable. We thank members of the University of Chicago Consortium on School Research's Steering Committee who commented on an earlier draft of this report—especially Peter Godard, Karen Lewis, and Luis Soria. It is always humbling to have our work critiqued by those with on-the-ground experience and we thank them for sharing that experience with us. Their thoughts helped shape this final product. Finally, we owe a deep debt of gratitude to members of the UChicago CCSR staff who worked with us as thought partners and readers through numerous iterations to arrive at this final report: The communications staff, Emily Krone and Bronwyn McDaniel, who kept us focused and offered excellent feedback; fellow researchers Elaine Allensworth, Jenny Nagaoka, Melissa Roderick, Penny Sebring, Marisa de la Torre, and Stuart Luppescu; and our superb final technical readers Lauren Sartain and Paul Moore. Our deep discussions with all of them have added to this report as well as our understanding of the promise and challenge of changing the teacher evaluation system in Chicago.

This report was produced by UChicago CCSR's publications and communications staff: Emily Krone, Director for Outreach and Communication; Bronwyn McDaniel, Communications and Research Manager; and Jessica Puller, Communications Specialist.

Graphic Design: Jeff Hall Design
Photography: Cynthia Howe and David Schalliol
Editing: Ann Lindner

09.2013/500/jh.design@rcn.com

Executive Summary

This report focuses on the perceptions and experiences of teachers and administrators during the first year of REACH implementation, which was in many ways a particularly demanding year. These experiences can be helpful to CPS and to other districts across the country as they work to restructure and transform teacher evaluation.

Historically, teacher evaluation in Chicago has fallen short on two crucial fronts: It has not provided administrators with measures that differentiated among strong and weak teachers—in fact, 93 percent of teachers were rated as Excellent or Superior—and it has not provided teachers with useful feedback they could use to improve their instruction.[1]

Chicago is not unique—teacher evaluation systems across the country have experienced the exact same problems.[2] Recent national policy has emphasized overhauling these systems to include multiple measures of teacher performance, such as student outcomes, and structuring the evaluations so they are useful from both talent management and teacher professional development perspectives. Principals and teachers need an evaluation system that provides teachers with specific, practice-oriented feedback they can use to improve their instruction and school leaders need to be able to identify strong and weak teachers. Required to act by a new state law and building off lessons learned from an earlier pilot of an evidence-based observation tool,[3] Chicago Public Schools (CPS) rolled out its new teacher evaluation system—Recognizing Educators Advancing Chicago's Students (REACH Students)—in the 2012-13 school year.

The REACH system seeks to provide a measure of individual teacher effectiveness that can simultaneously support instructional improvement. It incorporates teacher performance ratings based on multiple classroom observations together with student growth measured on two different types of assessments. While the practice of using classroom observations as an evaluation tool is not completely new, REACH requires teachers and administrators to conceptualize classroom observations more broadly as being part of instructional improvement efforts as well as evaluation; evaluating teachers based on student test score growth has never happened before in the district.

REACH implementation was a massive undertaking. It required a large-scale investment of time and energy from teachers, administrators, CPS central office staff, and the teachers union. District context played an important role and provided additional challenges as the district was introducing other major initiatives at the same time as REACH. Furthermore, the school year began with the first teacher strike in CPS in over 25 years. Teacher evaluation was one of several contentious points in the protracted negotiation, and the specific issue of using student growth on assessments to evaluate teachers received considerable coverage in the media.

This study uses data collected from fall 2012 through spring 2013, including:

- Two surveys of all 1,195 principals and assistant principals, administered in December 2012 and April/May 2013, respectively

- Two surveys of teachers, one administered in January 2013 to a sample of 2,000 classroom teachers and one administered in March 2013 to all teachers in the district

- Interviews with a random sample of 31 classroom teachers and six principals from six schools, conducted in spring 2013

- Interviews with nine central office staff members (Instructional Effectiveness Specialists), conducted in November 2012

Summary of Main Findings:

Teachers and administrators find the observation process useful for improving instruction

- Overwhelming majorities of teachers and administrators believe the observation process supports teacher growth, identifies areas of strength and weakness, and has improved the quality of professional conversations between them.

- Most administrators feel confident in their ability to gather evidence and assign ratings; a large majority of teachers believe their evaluator is fair and unbiased and able to assess their instruction.

- Some teachers expressed concern that classroom observation ratings are too subjective to be used in high-stakes evaluations, while others feel apprehensive about revealing instructional weaknesses for fear of being penalized on their evaluations.

Teachers are hesitant about the use of student growth on assessments to evaluate their classroom performance

- Over half of teachers surveyed believe REACH relies too heavily on student growth.

- Special education teachers are particularly critical and find the assessments to be inappropriate measures of their students' learning and their instruction.

Communication with teachers is an area for improvement; administrators want support on coaching and providing useful feedback

- The frequency and quality of training and communication received by teachers varies widely.

- Teachers are confused about how student growth factors into their final rating. Both teachers and administrators need clarity about score calculations and how they will be used for personnel decisions.

- Most administrators list coaching and providing useful feedback as high priorities for their own professional development.

REACH places demands on administrator time and capacity

- Administrators reported spending about six hours per formal observation cycle, including the observation, pre- and post-observation conferences, and data management. Based on the amount of time administrators reported spending on observations, and the average number of observations performed, the typical elementary school administrator spent approximately 120 hours—or two full weeks—solely on observations that were part of the teacher evaluation system. The typical high school administrator spent approximately three full weeks.

- Administrators are expected to train teachers about the system, conduct classroom observations, hold meaningful conversations with teachers about their instruction, and complete required paperwork while balancing their other job responsibilities.

This report is the first in a series of studies on Chicago's REACH teacher evaluation system. Subsequent work will investigate the consistency in observation ratings, the multiple measures of student growth, and the relationships among these variables. As the initiative continues to unfold, future work will also examine changes in these measures over time.

Introduction

In the fall of 2012, Chicago Public Schools (CPS) instituted a sweeping reform of its teacher evaluation system with the introduction of REACH Students. REACH Students replaces CPS's former 1970s–era checklist policy by incorporating a detailed classroom observation process and student growth measures into teachers' effectiveness scores (i.e., formal or summative evaluation ratings).[4]

With this policy, Chicago joins other states and districts across the country in developing new systems to evaluate teacher performance. More than 40 states now incorporate student test scores or other achievement measures into their teacher evaluations.[5] Over the next few years, several large urban districts (e.g., Los Angeles, Philadelphia, and New York) will be piloting or implementing similar new teacher evaluation systems required by their states.

This report provides an initial look at the first-year implementation of REACH (Recognizing Educators Advancing Chicago) Students (hereafter referred to as "REACH"). Recent reports on teacher evaluation have highlighted the problems that systems like Chicago's attempt to correct, but there is still much to learn about districts' implementation experiences and their early successes and challenges. We begin by describing the REACH evaluation system and the specific questions that guided our study.

Purpose and Design of REACH

Recent efforts to revamp teacher evaluation systems reflect the education field's increasing shift in focus from schools to individual teachers.[6] A growing number of studies are examining how student learning is related to teacher effectiveness. This work shows student achievement gains vary significantly across teachers. Furthermore, teacher effectiveness accounts for more

variation in student outcomes than any other school factor.[7] Policymakers have responded to these research findings: federal policy under the U.S. Department of Education's Race to the Top grant competition encourages states to identify strong and weak teachers by incorporating multiple measures of teacher performance in state evaluation requirements.[8] Combined, developments in education research and policy have put teacher effectiveness front-and-center of efforts to improve students' educational outcomes.

The possibility of receiving a federal Race to the Top grant prompted the Illinois State Board of Education to pursue key goals for providing students with access to high-quality teacher and leaders, and it incentivized Illinois legislators to pass the Performance Evaluation Reform Act (PERA) in 2010. PERA requires every district in Illinois to adopt new teacher evaluation systems that assess both teacher practice and student growth.[9] The teacher practice measures required by PERA must include multiple formal classroom observations, as well as support for teacher improvement. For student growth, the law defines various qualifying assessment types and combinations of assessments that must be used. Teacher performance and student growth ratings must then be combined to create a single, summative rating of teacher performance.

To comply with PERA requirements and to build off a generally successful pilot of an evidence-based observation rubric (see *CPS'S Experiment with Teacher Evaluation: EITP*, p. 8), CPS rolled out its new teacher evaluation system—REACH—in the 2012-13 school year. The main components of REACH in 2012-13 include:

- Multiple classroom observations: Non-tenured teachers must be observed four times per year, and observations must last for at least 45 minutes and include a pre- and post-observation conference. REACH requires administrators to provide feedback to teachers after each observation.

- An explicit observation rubric: REACH utilizes a modified version of the Charlotte Danielson Framework for Teaching.[10] In this rubric teachers are rated on four areas, or domains, of teaching practice: Planning and Preparation, Classroom Environment, Instruction, and Professional Responsibilities. Each of the domains is further broken down into 4-5 components in which expectations for each level of performance are described in detail.

- Trained evaluators: REACH requires all administrators to be certified by completing a series of training modules and passing two assessments. It further employs trained specialists that work with administrators on calibration and assigning evidence-based ratings aligned with the rubric.

- Student growth measures: REACH utilizes two different measures of student growth (Performance Tasks and either value-added or expected gains).

Although REACH is intended to provide a more accurate measurement of teacher practice, CPS has been clear that the system should also be a vehicle for professional growth. The CPS observation rubric (hereafter referred to as "the Framework") provides a common language about what constitutes effective teaching and a structure for having conversations focused on supporting instructional improvement (see Appendix B). Recent research on such process-based observations systems suggests that they can lead to improved student learning.[11] Furthermore, while test score data are intended to provide an additional measure of teacher effectiveness, they are also intended to inform teachers' choices about appropriate instructional content for their students.

REACH implementation was a massive undertaking. It required a large-scale investment of time and energy from teachers and administrators alike—in the form of training for administrators to be certified as observers, more frequent and time-intensive observations and conferences for both teachers and administrators, and overall training on a new and complex system. By the end of this year, the observation process had resulted in over 36,000 observations for about 6,000 non-tenured teachers and 13,000 tenured teachers. REACH also required the district to create a whole new set of assessments since many teachers do not teach in grade levels or subject areas that are captured on typical standardized assessments. In order to link students and teachers to provide accurate student growth information, the CPS central office had to redesign the way data on teachers and students are collected.

TABLE 1

CPS School and Personnel Statistics (2012-13)

Schools*	578
Elementary Schools	472
High Schools	106
Non-Tenured Teachers	5,743
Tenured Teachers	15,109
Administrators**	1,195

Source: CPS Stats and Facts, Administrative records

* Does not include charter or contract schools
** Only includes principals and assistant principals

The 2012-13 school year was particularly difficult time to launch such a large-scale and complex teacher evaluation system: The school year began with the first teacher strike in more than two decades; the CEO of CPS resigned in October, ushering in the third leadership change in four years; all schools had a longer day and year; and CPS began transitioning to the Common Core State Standards for teaching and learning. On top of all of this, debates about school closings, enrollment declines, and budget shortfalls began in the fall. A series of heavily attended and emotional public hearings were held throughout the year, and a controversial decision was made in the spring to close 49 schools.

Guiding Questions

The increased attention to teacher evaluation from policymakers and practitioners has been accompanied by increased attention from researchers seeking to evaluate implementation of these new systems. Many studies have focused on technical aspects, such as the reliability of the measurement tools.[12] Another important, but smaller, body of work has examined the use of new teacher evaluation systems in schools and districts.[13] Building on this early research, this report provides information on the first year of REACH implementation, answering questions about teachers' and administrators' perceptions of the system and their experiences with the new system. The specific questions and issues explored in this report include:

QUESTION 1: What are the benefits and drawbacks of observation systems designed for both teacher development and evaluation?

One of the benefits of using classroom observations in evaluation systems is that they have the potential to meet schools' dual needs of supporting professional growth and differentiating teacher practice.[14] Observations can create structures for providing teachers with timely and individualized feedback on their classroom practice. This information can guide coaching and professional development activities, as well as help teachers develop goals for improvement. In addition, observation ratings provide administrators with standardized and defensible evidence for making personnel decisions.

Yet, using observations for both purposes may also create a number of tensions. One study suggests that some teachers may be less likely to seek instructional support from administrators if exposing their weaknesses could result in a poor evaluation.[15] Furthermore, teachers may not respond positively to encouragement from administrators after receiving low ratings or disciplinary actions from them.[16] Finally, classroom evaluators who are responsible for supporting teacher growth and formally assessing effectiveness may introduce bias into the accountability process.[17] In short, if not implemented well, the benefits of using classroom observations may devolve into dueling purposes with each cancelling the benefits of the other.

UChicago CCSR's study of CPS's earlier pilot program, which was called the Excellence in Teaching Pilot, found that teachers and principals thought their discussions about instruction were more reflective and objective using the Danielson Framework than the CPS checklist.[18] Observations conducted under the pilot, however, did not count toward teachers' official evaluation score. In Chapter 1, we ask: How fair and useful do teachers and administrators find REACH classroom observations as a means of improving instruction? Does using school administrators as both coaches and evaluators raise any concerns or challenges?

QUESTION 2: How do teachers view the use of student growth on standardized assessments in their evaluation?

The incorporation of student growth measures into teachers' evaluations has been a contentious issue, both in Chicago and nationally. While supporters maintain teachers should be held accountable for student learning, critics contend that metrics designed to assess student progress are poor measures of teacher performance.[19] Additionally, opponents fear that adding stakes to student assessments increases the likelihood that teachers will narrow their curriculum or "teach to the test" so as to avoid a negative evaluation. Despite these issues, states and districts have moved forward with including student growth measures in teachers' evaluations.

Addressing teacher and administrator skepticism of student growth measures is critical for leveraging the full potential of the system to improve instruction. In Chapter 2, we ask: To what extent do teachers perceive student growth measures can provide an accurate assessment of their performance? How, if at all, are teachers using the assessment data produced by REACH?

QUESTION 3: What are the successes and challenges related to training and communication?

While REACH addresses many of the limitations of the previous teacher checklist system, thoughtful design is not enough to guarantee success.[20] Before REACH can improve teacher evaluation or instructional practice, it first has to move from a written policy document to a system embedded in the work of teachers and school

5

administrators. Implementation is critical to achieving intended outcomes.[21]

The task of implementing a teacher evaluation system of this scale and complexity should not be underestimated. REACH involves over 20,000 teachers and other school staff and 1,200 administrators in nearly 600 schools. Principals and assistant principals had to be certified and trained on using the new observation rubric. Teachers had to be informed about the goals of the new system, trained on how to engage in the new observation process, and taught how their summative evaluation score would be calculated. Observations and the pre- and post-observation conferences had to be scheduled and completed.

Understanding the experiences of teachers and administrators as they implemented such a complex and time-intensive system—in addition to all their other responsibilities—is a critical first step toward understanding any potential effects that REACH might have. If teachers and administrators are not informed of REACH's goals and do not understand its various elements, they may not implement the policy as intended. Insufficient training and resources are reasons for implementation failure.[22] In Chapter 3, we ask: How knowledgeable were teachers and administrators about REACH? How did they describe their training experiences? What aspects of implementation did participants identify as needing improvement?

QUESTION 4: How do principals understand and describe their capacity to manage classroom observation workloads?

In the last decade, principals have been increasingly called upon to be instructional leaders in their schools, especially through supporting effective instructional practices.[23] Given this emphasis on principals as instructional leaders, many assume that it is the principal who should be responsible for conducting observations and evaluating teacher practice.

It is not clear, however, whether principals have the time and capacity to manage the observation workload created by new evaluation systems. To increase the reliability of ratings, most systems call for teachers to be observed multiple times a year. Each observation typically involves scheduling and conducting the observation, writing up evidence and entering it into a database, having pre- and post-observation discussions with teachers, and coaching teachers on areas for improvement. The entire process for a single teacher can take several hours. While assistant principals in CPS also became certified evaluators, it still fell to the principals to ensure that all of the observations and pre- and post-conferences required by REACH were conducted.

Previous studies conducted by UChicago CCSR researchers have highlighted some of the capacity issues created by the introduction of new teacher evaluation systems. For example, workload demands contributed to lower engagement in the new system for some principals, while others reported giving less attention to tenured teachers in order to complete all of their required evaluations.[24] In Chapter 4, we ask: How much time did administrators spend on classroom observations during the first year of REACH? How do they feel about the demands the new REACH system places on them?

In This Report

Chapters 1 and 2 of this report describe the observation and student growth elements of REACH and provide participants' perceptions about the value of this initiative as both an evaluation and development tool. Chapters 3 and 4 describe participants' experiences with implementation, focusing on communication, training, and time demands. Finally, in Chapter 5, we present some questions to consider as implementation continues. Additional reports in this series will investigate observation ratings, student growth ratings, and the relationship between them.

What Goes Into a Teacher's Evaluation Score?

A teacher's REACH summative evaluation score is comprised of a teacher practice score and up to two measures of student growth. The teacher practice component consists of classroom observations completed by a certified administrator utilizing the CPS Framework for Teaching, a modified version of the Danielson Framework for Teaching. Student growth measures are discussed in detail in Chapter 2. In 2012-13 only non-tenured teachers were to receive a summative evaluation score.

Elementary Teachers in Tested Subjects/Grades
(Receive individual value-added)

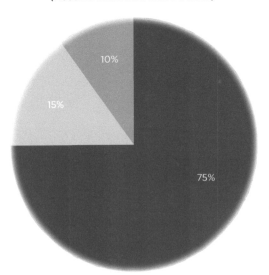

Elementary Teachers in Untested Subjects/Grades
(Receive schoolwide value-added in literacy)

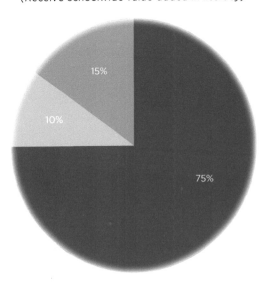

High School Teachers in Core Subject Areas

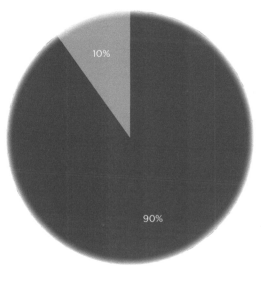

High School Teachers in Non-Core Subject Areas

■ Teacher Practice: CPS Framework for Teaching
■ Student Growth: REACH Performance Tasks
□ Student Growth: Value-Added

Source: Chicago Public Schools

To answer our questions we used multiple sources of information, including surveys and interviews. Surveys provide a broad picture of participants' perceptions; interviews provide deeper insights into participants' experiences.

- **Winter 2012-13 Surveys:** We surveyed all 1,195 principals and assistant principals in December 2012, receiving 733 responses (a 61 percent response rate). We surveyed a random sample of 1,000 non-tenured teachers and 1,000 tenured teachers in January 2013.[A] We received 901 responses (a 45 percent response rate). The entire content of this survey administration was related to REACH.

- **Spring 2013 Surveys:** We included survey items as part of CPS's annual My Voice, My School survey. This survey was administered to all teachers in March 2013 and had a response rate of 81 percent. Then, we surveyed all principals and assistant principals in April/May 2013, receiving 687 responses (a 57 percent response rate). Some questions were the same as in the winter 2012 survey to gauge changes in perception; others were different because the initiative was more mature. Survey content was shared with other topics.

- **Spring 2013 Principal and Teacher Interviews:** We randomly selected three high schools and five elementary schools for our interview sample. We then randomly selected teachers from within those schools to interview. We were able to interview six principals and 31 classroom teachers from six schools.

- **Fall 2012 CPS Central Office Staff (Instructional Effectiveness Specialists) Interviews:** We interviewed nine specialists (about half of the staff in this position) in November 2012. These specialists were charged with providing technical assistance to administrators in conducting classroom observations.

CPS's Experiment with Teacher Evaluation: EITP

Between 2008 and 2010 CPS implemented the Excellence in Teaching Pilot (EITP), a pilot teacher evaluation program that used the Charlotte Danielson Framework for Teaching to guide the evaluation of classroom instruction. EITP provided an alternative system to the teacher evaluation checklist CPS had used for 30 years. Over the two-year period, a total of 100 elementary schools participated in the pilot.

CPS's current REACH evaluation system resembles EITP in many ways. Like the pilot, trained administrator evaluators observe teachers' classroom instruction using a modified version of the Danielson Framework. Some observations are unannounced and others are planned in advance and include a pre- and post-observation conference. The new system, however, differs from EITP on several important dimensions. First, although the pilot had no stakes attached, REACH is the official evaluation system for non-tenured teachers in its first year, and will expand to include stakes for all teachers over time. Second, while administrator training for the smaller-scale pilot was done in-person, training for the new system was provided statewide via an online platform. And finally, the pilot provided measures of performance based only on observations, while the new system includes a student growth component for all teachers regardless of the grade or subject they teach.

UChicago CCSR's two-year study of the pilot found most principals and teachers were supportive of EITP and found it beneficial for their practice. Specifically, principals and teachers reported using the Danielson Framework and evidence from classroom observations made their conversations about instruction more objective and reflective. In addition, the study found principals' ratings of teachers were both valid and reliable.[B] The pilot also uncovered some challenges. For example, many principals lacked the instructional coaching skills required to have deep discussions about teaching practice. Where principals were less proficient at conferencing with teachers, teachers were less positive about the new system and more doubtful of their principal's ability to use the Framework accurately or rate them fairly. A later follow-up study of EITP found that the pilot had a positive effect on both reading and math scores. Higher-achieving schools and those serving fewer low-income students were the primary beneficiaries.[C]

CHAPTER 1

The Classroom Observation Process

The main element of the REACH evaluation system is the observation process used to rate teacher practice. The process is centered around the CPS Framework for Teaching (the Framework), a classroom observation rubric based on the Charlotte Danielson Framework (see Appendix B). REACH also establishes a set of procedures for how evaluators should conduct classroom observations, collect evidence about what was observed, and discuss the evidence and ratings with teachers (see Table 2).

The teacher practice component is intended to serve two functions. Drawing on its roots in the Danielson Framework, the classroom observation process is structured to provide teachers with information they can use to improve their teaching practices. It includes a pre- and post-observation conference to create a forum for evaluators to provide constructive feedback to teachers on their practice and offer support for improvement. In addition, the teacher practice component is intended to provide school administrators with a means to evaluate the instructional effectiveness of

teachers in their building. Ratings across classroom observations are combined with test score gains to give each teacher an official evaluation score.

In this chapter we examine teachers' and administrators' perceptions of the teacher practice component. Our findings draw on both survey and interview data. Survey data show the extent to which teachers and principals across the district have positive or negative views about the observations process. Overall, both groups find the process to be a useful means of helping teachers improve their instructional practice. Teachers appreciate the feedback they receive from their evaluators and believe the rating process is transparent. Administrators think the observation process will lead to improvements in teaching and student learning. Interview data provide insight into how the observation process supports instructional improvement. In addition, it highlights teachers' descriptions of how the coordination of the evaluation process can undermine the value of the observations as an improvement tool.

9

TABLE 2

What does the formal observation process include in 2012-13?

Pre-Observation Conference	Classroom Observation	Post-Observation Conference
• A brief 15-20 minute conference with a focus on Domain 1 (Planning and Preparation) • The teacher and administrator decide which lesson will be evaluated	• The administrator observes teacher for about 45 minutes • Observation primarily focuses on the components in Domain 2 (Classroom Environment) and Domain 3 (Instruction) • The administrator gathers evidence and assigns ratings	• The teacher and administrator discuss the classroom observation • The teacher's self-reflection is evaluated for Component 4A (Reflecting on Teaching and Learning) • Ends with suggestions for improving teacher practice

Source: Modified from *REACH Students Teacher Practice*

Note: In 2012-13 administrators were required to conduct at least four formal observations for each non-tenured teacher and at least one formal observation for each tenured teacher.

The Observation Process Supports Professional Growth

Administrators and teachers expressed positive views of the teacher practice component's potential to support teacher growth and professional development. On the survey, 76 percent of teachers said the evaluation process at their school encourages their professional growth. Similarly, 76 percent of administrators reported believing that the observation process would result in instructional improvement at their school, and 82 percent reported noticeable improvements in half or more of the teachers they had observed over the school year (**see Figure 1**).

In interviews, teachers identified three ways in which the observation component supports teacher learning. First, they remarked that the Framework rubric sets clear expectations about quality instruction. As one teacher succinctly put it: *"The observation rubric describes what really good teaching looks like. It gives me a clear description of what teaching looks like at each level."* Responses on surveys indicate that many teachers and administrators agree with this sentiment:

75 percent of teachers and 91 percent of administrators reported that the Framework provides a common definition of high-quality and effective teaching. Clear descriptions of quality instruction help teachers transcend their own individual opinions about teaching and begin to compare their practice to others. One teacher explained:

> You get into your own practices and form your habits and methods. But because everyone is working within the REACH system, you can start to see where you are in the system. Everyone is breathing the system language. If they all are reflecting the same language, you have to think about others and all the other teachers.

Because it creates explicit and shared expectations of quality instruction, teachers and administrators commented that the rubric also provides clear guidance about what teachers need to address in order to improve their practice:

> I always thought there needed to be higher standards in teaching, and I think the observation rubric has made the standards higher. [Before] it was up to the principal's discretion of how he or she felt. [Now] it's clearer about what that means, how to grow, how to improve. —CPS Teacher

> [In post-conferences] instead of just saying, 'You got a 3 here and a 2 here,' we can say, 'What is the difference between a basic and proficient [rating]? I didn't see this, I didn't see this.' And it was a really clear thing, 'Start doing that,' or, 'Stop doing something else.' —CPS Principal

Administrators were virtually unanimous on this point: 96 percent responded on the winter survey that the Framework helps them identify areas where teachers can improve.

Second, teachers reported that the teacher practice component has potential to improve instruction

FIGURE 1

Most administrators report at least half of their teachers have incorporated feedback and improved

Of the teachers you have observed this year, how many...

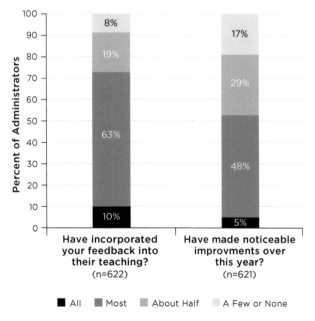

Source: Spring Administrator Survey, May 2013

Note: Percentages may not add up to 100 due to rounding.

10

because it creates opportunities to discuss teaching with administrators and colleagues. In particular, the pre- and post-conferences were a way of getting needed feedback and support:

> I love being able to refine what I do and talk about it with somebody. So the idea is that I get to sit down every month or so and say 'this isn't really working for me' and my administrator will find something that can help me. That is really beneficial.
> —CPS Teacher

> I think that it is nice to have someone in the classroom frequently to really see how you're doing and what you're doing and give you feedback in a way that is not really an attack. It's more like a positive, constructive criticism on different aspects of teaching. —CPS Teacher

These comments highlight that teachers value feedback on their instruction. They also show that conversations with administrators tend to be respectful and supportive. In fact, only 6 percent of teachers on the winter survey said feedback was delivered in a hurtful manner. Across the district, 82 percent of teachers indicated they have professional conversations with their administrators focused on instruction, 89 percent said their evaluator supports their growth, and 76 percent reported that their evaluator's feedback was useful. Among administrators, 94 percent thought the Framework has improved the quality of their conversations with teachers about instruction.

Finally, teachers also noted the conversations helped them intentionally reflect on their own classroom practice. *"I think it's good to see what you did and how you can improve,"* one teacher said. *"I can't see myself teach, and I love to hear how I can improve."* By creating opportunities to examine their own practice, the observation process helps teachers identify their strengths and weaknesses, as well as prioritize areas on which to focus their improvement efforts. For some, the reflection habit carries outside of the

formal observation structure to their teaching more generally: *"[The Framework] causes us to be more conscious of our planning and the words coming out of our mouth. It causes us to really look at what we are doing in our classrooms."*

Administrators agreed: 92 percent of principal and assistant principal survey respondents thought the Framework encourages teachers in their school to reflect on their instructional practice (**see Figure 2**). On the winter survey, 81 percent of teachers said it helps them identify areas where their teaching is strong, and 82 percent said it helps them identify areas where they can improve.

Most Teachers Believe Administrator Ratings were Accurate and Fair

Teachers were generally positive about the accuracy of the ratings they received from school administrators. On the spring survey, 87 percent of teachers said their evaluator was fair and unbiased, and 88 percent said they were able to assess their instruction accurately (**see Figure 3**). On the winter survey, 72 percent of teachers said their ratings were about the same or higher than they thought they should have been.

One reason teachers were positive about their ratings is they believe the specificity of the Framework helps makes ratings more concrete:

> I like that they [the Framework] actually specify what it is that we are being evaluated on, versus the old system where your principal essentially gave you a rating and some comments about what you've been doing. With this [system], you're either doing this or you're not. If you're not, then you're not meeting [the standards]. If you are, then you're proficient.

Another reason teachers feel ratings tend to be generally objective is because administrators have to collect and present evidence about what they specifically saw during observations. *"[The Framework] holds a lot of accountability,"* one teacher said. *"Not only for the teachers but also for the administrator; they have to prove everything they've found."*

FIGURE 2

Nearly all administrators report the CPS Framework is useful for instructional improvement

The CPS Framework...

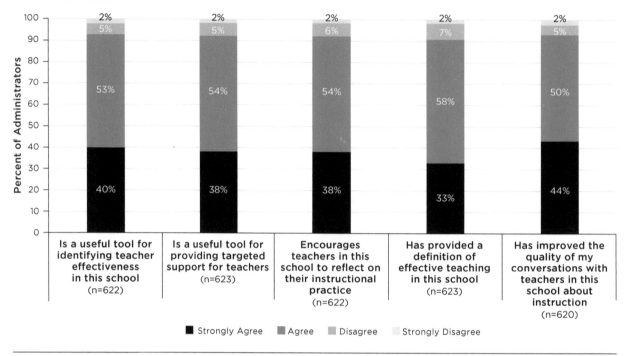

■ Strongly Agree ■ Agree ■ Disagree ■ Strongly Disagree

Source: Spring Administrator Survey, May 2013

Note: Percentages may not add up to 100 due to rounding.

FIGURE 3

Most teachers believe their evaluator has the capacity to assess instruction fairly and accurately

My evaluator...

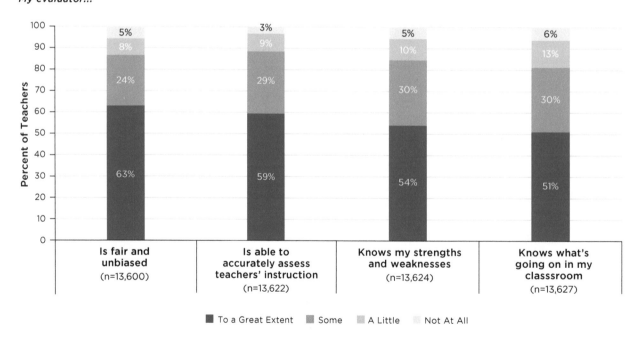

■ To a Great Extent ■ Some ■ A Little ■ Not At All

Source: Spring Teacher Survey MVMS, April 2013

Note: Percentages may not add up to 100 due to rounding.

While having positive perceptions of their rating, some teachers thought using multiple raters could improve the reliability of the ratings and how they are used in personnel decisions. One concern is that being observed by only one evaluator may lead to inaccurate ratings. Recent research seems to validate this view, finding that multiple observers produce more reliable ratings.[25] *"I think it would be something to think about... having each observation done by a second person,"* one teacher stated. *"Yes, ratings are evidence based, but [evaluators] do make interpretations based on previous knowledge of you. So I think that ties into how they view what you are doing and if you are doing it well."*

In addition, some teachers worry administrators may use observation ratings to remove or deny tenure to staff they do not like. Thus, the ratings one receives may have little to do with what actually happens during an observation. *"I just feel like it shouldn't be the administration who is doing the observation on you,"* one teacher said. *"Because the bottom line is that if they don't want to keep you in the school, they are not going to. They are going to give you a bad observation rating."* Some cities have addressed this problem by incorporating governance structures that support personnel systems. These systems typically include the use of expert mentor teachers as evaluators and coaches, as well as review structures for personnel decisions that involve teachers and administrators in the decision-making process.[26]

Administrators' Dual Role Can Undermine Professional Learning Benefits

REACH's reliance on administrators both to officially evaluate teacher practice and to provide instructional coaching may undermine the learning potential of the observation process. Because observation ratings have such a big impact on summative evaluation scores, teachers are highly motivated to demonstrate their professional competence when they are observed. Since the administrator giving official ratings is simultaneously providing instructional support, however, teachers are forced to weigh the costs and benefits of using the observation process as an opportunity to share their instructional weaknesses. For some teachers, the risk of receiving a poor rating is too great. As one teacher explained:

Because there is such an emphasis placed on assessing the quality of teachers, there is no incentive for teachers to admit insecurity or talk about areas in which he or she struggles. I felt like I had to mask the things that I didn't do as well and try to explain why they didn't go well because, at the end of the day, I'm being rated. So there is more of an incentive to present myself favorably than to have an honest discussion about instruction.

Several teachers across our interviews schools described instances when they perceived that attempts to get support for addressing weaknesses led to negative consequences on their evaluation. For example, one teacher said he was very honest at the start of the year about his practice by highlighting for his evaluator *"things in my daily teaching that I need to strive to fix."* After being informally warned that his evaluator would pay more attention to those areas, he felt as though the evaluator:

...ended up putting a laser focus on the things that I do want to fix, but are hard to fix. Instead of being rewarded for being self-aware and honest about improvements, I feel like I'm actually being penalized.

Another teacher recounted going to her principal for help regarding classroom management issues in one class. Instead of receiving support, she felt the request led to her receiving a low observation rating:

My principal joked around and said he'll do my next observation in that classroom [in which I was struggling]. It was a joke, and then he actually did it. When I said I really don't know if it is appropriate for me to be judged based on that classroom, when there are so many other classrooms and grades that I teach where I've already been observed, I was scolded and told that I am essentially saying that I can't do my job...It makes me feel like I can't even come to my own administrator for help, because that information was essentially used against me in the observation process.

These two comments highlight the potential risks involved in asking an evaluator for support. If teachers present a realistic view of their teaching, they may be rated as less skilled compared to others who put on a *"performance"* during a scheduled observation. It is important to keep in mind that we do not have evidence about how widespread instances like the ones above are. Nonetheless, these cautions show how the learning opportunities created by the observation process could, in the long run, be undermined when the evaluators giving ratings are also primary instructional coaches.

14

CHAPTER 2

The Use of Student Growth in Evaluation

Prior to REACH, teachers in Chicago were not held formally accountable for the performance of their students. The use of student growth to measure teacher performance breaks new ground. A teacher's student growth score summarizes the change in his or her students' standardized test scores between two time periods: under REACH, the beginning and end of a school year.[27] PERA requires that student growth be a "significant factor" in teachers' evaluations, though CPS and the CTU agreed to phase in this requirement so that student growth accounted for no more than 25 percent of a teacher's evaluation score in the initial year. The weight given to student growth in a teacher's final evaluation varies according to the subject and grade level of the teacher (see *What Goes Into a Teacher's Evaluation Score?* on **p. 7**). Student growth is calculated differently depending on the assessment that is used. These assessments also vary by grade and subject, but they can include:

- A gain score on district-developed Performance Tasks, which are written or hands-on assessments specifically designed for the grade and subject of the course and are most often scored by the teacher

- A value-added score on the NWEA MAP, an adaptive, computer-based test administered to students in grades 3-8 in reading and math

- An expected gains score on the subject area EXPLORE, PLAN, or ACT (EPAS) assessments administered to students in grades 9-11 in English, reading, math, and science[28]

- A measure of average schoolwide literacy growth from either the NWEA MAP or the EPAS

The Student Growth Component of REACH box on page 20 further describes the measures of student growth used in REACH.

As set forth by PERA, student growth is incorporated strictly for evaluation purposes. However, CPS has been clear that they expect REACH to positively affect teacher development and student learning. If the student growth component is to be useful beyond teachers' evaluations, it must provide teachers with information that can inform their instruction. A student growth score alone does not provide teachers with information that is timely or detailed enough to guide improvements in their instructional practice; it is one number that summarizes changes in test scores across a group of students over a given period of time. In contrast, students' performance on the individual assessments used to calculate student growth might inform teachers' instruction by providing them with information on their students' skills or level of understanding.

In this chapter, we describe teachers' responses to the use of student growth in their evaluations, as well as how useful teachers found the assessments for their instruction. We find apprehension among teachers about the incorporation of student growth metrics into their evaluation. Teachers were generally positive about the potential instructional value of the assessments used to measure student growth, though the perceived usefulness varied considerably by the assessment.

Teachers Are Apprehensive About the Use of Student Growth in Their Evaluation

Given that student growth is a new addition to teachers' evaluation, it is not surprising that many teachers expressed concerns over its use in measuring teacher performance and in personnel decisions, or that many were misinformed or confused about how student growth factors into their evaluation. Additionally, some teachers raised concerns about the potential for bias when applying the student growth measures across different classroom contexts.

On our survey, 57 percent of teachers said that they believe or strongly believe that the REACH system relies too heavily on standardized tests (**see Figure 4**). Another 30 percent said that they somewhat believe

15

this, while only 13 percent of teachers said that they do not believe that REACH relies too heavily on standardized tests. We asked teachers an open-ended question about what they found most problematic about the REACH system. Nearly one-third of the 552 teachers who responded to this question identified the student growth component and the assessments used to measure student growth, making these the most frequently cited problematic aspects of REACH.[29] While some of these teachers maintained that test scores should never be used in teachers' evaluations, others identified more specific concerns. These concerns included the narrow representation of student learning that is measured by standardized tests, the numerous influences on student performance that are outside of a teacher's control, and an increase in the already heavy testing burden on teachers and students.[30]

Teachers' responses to our interview and an open-ended survey item revealed that many of them were misinformed or unclear on how much student growth contributes to their summative evaluation. For example, one teacher wrote, *"I am concerned about my effort as a teacher completely relying on the test scores of my*

FIGURE 4

Most teachers believe or strongly believe REACH relies too heavily on standardized tests

Please indicate the extent to which you believe that REACH, overall, relies too heavily on standardized tests.

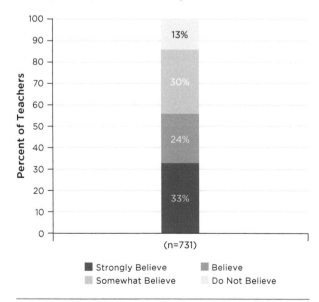

(n=731)

■ Strongly Believe   ■ Believe
■ Somewhat Believe   ■ Do Not Believe

Source: Winter Teacher Survey, January 2013
Note: Percentages may not add up to 100 due to rounding.

students." In fact, student growth does not account for more than 25 percent of any teacher's evaluation this year, and student growth will not account for more than 30 percent once REACH is fully implemented; therefore, no teacher's evaluation will *completely* rely on test scores. Some teachers further attributed the incorporation of student growth to the district, rather than to the state law. As we show in the next chapter, most teachers reported receiving information about REACH from their school administration. Yet only 45 percent of principals and assistant principals reported having a strong or very strong understanding of how student growth factors into a teacher's summative rating, so it is not surprising that teachers are also unclear.

Several teachers expressed concerns that measures of student growth are unfair to teachers in more challenging schools because student growth, and therefore a teacher's evaluation score, is related to the supports that students may or may not receive outside of the classroom. One teacher explained this concern:

> ... I'm not going to want to work in a [struggling] school if my evaluation is tied to test scores, because there are things that I can't control. I can't stop gang violence. I can't stop poverty. I can't stop the parents who don't care if their kids go to school. I think the part that I find unfair is that so much of what goes on in these kids' lives is affecting their academics, and those are things that a teacher cannot possibly control.

Related to the issue of fairness, many teachers expressed apprehension over how the student growth measures would be used by the district— in particular that they would be used to fire teachers or to institute merit pay. For example, one teacher explained that she had *"grave concerns"* that her students' performance could negatively impact her job security, in part because there are so many other factors outside of the classroom that influence student growth.

Two groups of teachers—special education teachers and non-core subject teachers—were particularly critical of the student growth component. Special education teachers raised concerns that

16

the REACH Performance Tasks, NWEA MAP, and EPAS assessments were inappropriate measures of their instruction and of their students' learning. One special education teacher explained: *"The grade level REACH Performance Tasks were nearly impossible for my special education students, and it will be difficult to show improvement for many students who are four and five grade levels behind."* This teacher's concern was echoed by many special education teachers who believed that holding their students—and, therefore, their own evaluation—to the same standard as regular education students and teachers was unfair. Many teachers were unclear on what accommodations could be provided for their special education students as they took the assessments, which were the same assessments that were given to regular education students.[31]

Some non-core subject teachers (e.g., art, music, and physical education) were troubled by the incorporation of schoolwide literacy growth into their evaluation. These teachers disliked being held accountable for the work of other teachers and for a content area that they were not necessarily prepared to teach. For example, a high school art teacher explained his feelings about the schoolwide literacy measure:

> The comment has been made that I will get judged on reading scores because we are all teachers of literacy, and there's a part of me that agrees with that. But...there is no part of my certification or training that says I need to learn how to teach a student how to read.

Teachers Found Beginning-of-Year REACH Performance Tasks Useful

The REACH Performance Tasks were developed by teachers and district specialists as Type III assessments (see *The Student Growth Component of REACH* on p. 20). As defined by PERA, Type III assessments are rigorous, aligned to the course's curriculum, and measure student learning in that course. Performance Tasks are *"a written or hands-on demonstration of mastery, or progress towards mastery, of a particular skill or standard,"*[32] which make them very different from traditional multiple-choice assessments. The primary purpose of the REACH Performance Tasks is to provide

a measure of student understanding at the beginning and end of the school year so that a growth score can be calculated and incorporated into teachers' evaluations. In the best case, however, the beginning-of-year Performance Tasks would also provide teachers with information that is useful for their instruction, such as information about their students' skills or about the district's expectations for what content should be covered in their class.

Among teachers who administered a beginning-of-year REACH Performance Task, 70 percent reported that it was somewhat or very useful for their instruction (see Figure 5). In interviews, teachers reported using the Performance Tasks as an indication of what material they needed to cover. Moreover, teachers seemed to appreciate the more comprehensive set of skills that students could demonstrate on the Performance Tasks: 72 percent agreed that the tasks provided information that is not measured on traditional multiple-choice assessments.

While the Performance Tasks provided teachers with insight into what material they needed to cover, few teachers used the Performance Tasks as measures of student understanding. Two-thirds of teachers (67 percent) agreed that the Performance Tasks were rigorous assessments of student learning, but they may have been too rigorous; nearly the same proportion (66 percent) indicated that the tasks were too challenging for beginning-of-year assessments. Because the Performance Tasks often covered material that the students had not yet been exposed to, they did not provide a measure of students' understanding of that material. Rather than test students' prior knowledge, the Performance Tasks assessed students on content that they had not been taught. One teacher explained why the level of challenge is particularly a problem for a beginning-of-year assessment:

> ...[my students] were really upset by it. Not only because it was something they had never seen before, but they didn't know me, so it was kind of like they didn't know me and I was giving them something and challenging them in a way that it was unfair for them and it made me feel really bad.

This teacher explained that once she has gotten to know her students, she can motivate them to persevere through a challenging assessment. But without the time to build those relationships, it was difficult for her to help her students overcome their frustration.

There was fairly widespread confusion among teachers about the administration of the Performance Tasks. Just 41 percent of teachers who had administered a beginning-of-year Performance Task indicated that they were clear on how the tasks should be scored. Over one-third (36 percent) of teachers indicated they did not have adequate time to score the tasks, and one-third (35 percent) indicated they had difficulty recording the scores on the district's internal site. Just under half (43 percent) of teachers indicated that they were not at all clear on what accommodations could be made for students with IEPs who were taking a Performance Task.

Apart from their instructional value, several teachers raised concerns about how easy it would be to game the scoring of the Performance Tasks. Teachers score their own students' Performance Tasks at both the beginning and end of the year. In an interview and on an open-ended survey item, teachers noted that if they wanted to maximize their student growth score, they could simply give all students a low score on the beginning-of-year task and a higher score at the end of the year. While we have no measures of how frequently—if at all—this practice occurred, it has the potential to undermine how teachers and administrators perceive the accuracy of the evaluation ratings.

NWEA MAP Provided Timely and Useful Data

The NWEA MAP is a series of computer-based, adaptive assessments administered to CPS students in grades 3-8 at the beginning and end of the school year.[33] Seventy-eight percent of teachers who administered a beginning-of-year NWEA MAP assessment found it somewhat or very useful for their instruction (**see Figure 5**) and a similar proportion (75 percent) agreed that the NWEA MAP helped them to target their instruction to meet students' individual needs.

FIGURE 5

Teachers report assessments vary in instructional usefulness

How useful is the following for your instruction?

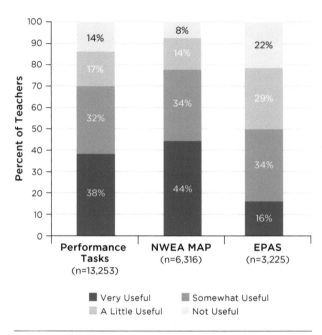

Source: Spring Teacher Survey MVMS, April 2013

Note: Responses only include teachers who conducted the assessment(s) in the fall of 2012. Only high school teachers in core subjects administered EPAS. Only elementary school teachers in grades 3-8 reading and math administered NWEA MAP. All elementary school teachers and a subset of high school teachers in core subjects administered Performance Tasks. Percentages may not add up to 100 due to rounding.

The rigor of the NWEA MAP assessments and the timeliness with which teachers receive their students' results may help to explain the NWEA MAP's instructional value. Eighty-five percent of teachers who had administered the beginning-of-year NWEA MAP found it to be a rigorous assessment of student learning. Additionally, the majority of teachers agreed that the results provided by the NWEA MAP are both timely (92 percent) and easy to understand and use (72 percent).

While the computerized nature of the NWEA MAP assessments likely contributed to their instructional usefulness, it also created problems for some teachers. Over two-thirds of teachers who had administered the beginning-of-year NWEA MAP reported that they experienced technical difficulties, such as issues with computer hardware or internet access. One teacher explained how technical problems can affect student performance:

At our school, our technology isn't up-to-date. The computers themselves are about nine or 10 years old....When everybody was taking the test at once, that was an issue because our routers couldn't handle the amount of traffic. So the internet would go out. I think that really skewed our test results because students, especially on reading, would have to read the story and then go back to it and then they were stuck and they would have to go back. The students won't reread what they read, so they might forget a part, and then they're asked questions.

How to use the NWEA MAP with particular populations of students was again a concern for teachers: 30 percent were not at all clear on what accommodations were acceptable for special education students and 39 percent were not at all clear on whether ELL students should take the NWEA MAP.

EPAS Results Not Timely or Detailed

High school teachers were less positive about the value of the beginning-of-year EPAS assessments for their instruction than elementary teachers were about the NWEA MAP assessments. EPAS assessments are given in grades 9-11, as part of ACT's testing system. While 71 percent of teachers who had administered a beginning-of-year EPAS assessment agreed that the test was a rigorous assessment of student learning, only 50 percent of those teachers reported that it was somewhat useful or very useful for their instruction (**see Figure 5**).

One issue limiting the instructional value of the beginning-of-year EPAS assessments is the timeliness with which teachers receive their results. Unlike the computer-based NWEA MAP that provides teachers with results immediately following the assessment, teachers do not receive their students' EPAS scores for several months. Just 50 percent of teachers who administered a beginning-of-year EPAS assessment indicated that they had received their students' results in a timely manner. In our interviews, we heard why this delay is problematic for teachers:

We didn't get the results back until basically almost January, so it's kind of like the data is dead...[it] reflected what they knew three months ago. If I had gotten an item analysis, that would have been more helpful. But I just got a raw score so I know that they scored a 14....I know I want to improve that score, but I don't know why they're getting that score.

Moreover, as the teacher above explained, the results of the EPAS exams are not detailed enough to guide teachers' instruction.[34] Teachers receive their students' subject scores, but not an item analysis. Just 44 percent of teachers indicated that the beginning-of-year EPAS helped them to pinpoint individual students' strengths and weaknesses.

Since high schools had administered EPAS as paper and pencil exams for a number of years before the implementation of REACH, their administration caused less widespread confusion among teachers than the NWEA MAP or REACH Performance Tasks. However, the issue of how to use the tests with special education and ELL students remained: 25 percent of teachers indicated that they were not at all clear on what accommodations were acceptable for students with IEPs and 35 percent were unclear on whether their ELL students should take the assessment.

As this chapter and the one that precedes it show, the implementation of the observation process and student growth component of REACH required substantial effort from teachers and administrators. In the next chapter, we explore the challenges and successes of training and communication to support this effort.

Illinois' Performance Evaluation Reform Act (PERA) defines three different assessment types:

- Type I assessments can be the typical multiple-choice standardized assessment that "measures a certain group or subset of students in the same manner with the same potential assessment items, is scored by a non-district entity, and is administered either state-wide or beyond Illinois."

- Type II assessments can be "any assessment developed or adopted and approved for use by the school district and used on a district-wide basis by all teachers in a given grade or subject area."

- Type III assessments are "rigorous, aligned to the course's curriculum," and are determined by the teacher and qualified evaluator to measure student learning in that course.[D]

PERA stipulates that all teachers must be evaluated using at least one Type I or Type II assessment and at least one Type III assessment.[E] To meet this requirement, CPS has identified two different types of student assessments to be used as part of REACH:

REACH Performance Tasks

As its Type III assessment, CPS utilizes REACH Performance Tasks, which were administered in the fall and the spring and are intended to measure change in student mastery over one or two skills or standards. The REACH Performance Tasks were developed by over 150 teachers organized into teams aided by content area specialists from central office. These teams developed over 90 Performance Tasks that covered all elementary teachers, including those teaching in areas such as art, music, physical education, and library studies that are not traditionally covered by standardized tests and a subset of teachers in high school core courses. Each Performance Task fall/spring pair took approximately 40 hours to draft, revise, and pilot.

Value-Added and Expected Gains Measures

For its Type I assessment in elementary schools, CPS has chosen to compute teachers' value-added score on the math and reading NWEA MAP. A value-added score from the fall to spring administrations of the NWEA MAP will be computed for teachers who teach grades three through eight reading or math. All other elementary school teachers will receive a schoolwide literacy growth score.

For its Type I assessment for high school teachers, CPS is exploring using the EPAS suite of tests (EXPLORE, PLAN, and ACT) to measure expected student gains. In 2012-13, the EPAS assessments were administered without stakes. EXPLORE was administered twice to ninth-graders, PLAN twice to tenth -graders, and ACT twice to eleventh-graders. While these scores will not count towards teachers' evaluation this year, the data will be used to develop an expected gains metric for possible use in the 2013-14 school year.

CHAPTER 3

Training and Communication

As with the implementation of any major policy initiative, REACH required extensive communication and training efforts at both the district and school levels. In Chicago, almost 1,200 administrators and over 20,000 teachers needed to be informed about and trained on the new system in this first year of implementation.

In this chapter, we describe teacher and administrator experiences with training and communication. We draw upon our surveys and interviews of teachers and administrators to understand how well-informed and prepared participants felt in this first year of implementation, and to explore what areas they felt still needed improvement. We find that, while administrators received extensive training, training and information for teachers varied widely both across and within schools. Finally, teachers and administrators alike expressed a need for transparency not only about how final summative scores would be calculated but also about how teacher evaluation would ultimately be utilized in personnel decisions.

Administrators Felt Prepared to Conduct Observations and Assign Ratings

More than 80 percent of administrators reported their proficiency as strong or very strong in recording and aligning evidence and determining observation ratings. Administrators received extensive training in these areas. Prior to conducting any observations, administrators had to complete an online certification process that included video-based scoring practice and an assessment of their rating accuracy. On average, administrators reported spending over 30 hours on this certification process. Administrators who did not pass the assessment portion of this certification after two attempts were required to attend additional in-person training. Administrators who did not pass the assessment portion after four attempts did not conduct observations. As of November 2012, almost 90 percent of CPS administrators had been certified.[35]

Beyond certification, the district required administrators to attend four half-day, foundational REACH professional development sessions throughout the year. These sessions included content on the teacher practice component, evidence alignment, rating calibration, and evidence-based conversations. On our administrator survey, about 70 percent of administrators said they found district-provided professional development on REACH helpful or very helpful.

In interviews, administrators reported conducting joint observations with another practitioner and discussing the evidence and ratings they assigned was most relevant to helping them feel prepared. Administrators often relied on their network's Instructional Effectiveness Specialist for this on-the-job training and were positive about the individualized coaching they received (see *Instructional Effectiveness Specialists*). Over

Instructional Effectiveness Specialists

Specialists conduct joint classroom observations and calibration sessions with administrators in their schools. Specialist ratings are not directly incorporated into any teachers' evaluation rating. Instead their purpose is to work with administrators on their ability to assign unbiased ratings based only on the evidence they collected during observations.

In 2012-13 there were 18 specialists, approximately one for every school network (although some were not hired by the time school started in the fall). Individual specialists' backgrounds, experiences and capacity varied, but all were certified and trained to ensure evaluator quality and inter-rater reliability as well as identify evaluators' needs in conducting observations.

80 percent of administrators found their conversations with their network specialist helpful or very helpful in the areas of evidence collection, alignment, and assignment of ratings. In interviews, principals stated they found conducting joint observations with their specialist helpful because they could focus on their individual needs as observers.

Principals also relied heavily on their own administrative teams for training and calibration. In our interviews, principals reported spending significant time training, jointly observing, comparing evidence, and discussing ratings with their assistant principals at the beginning of the year. One principal and assistant principal team even planned to conduct all of their observations together because they felt it would maximize their learning and ensure calibration:

> We did them together because we wanted to coordinate and do what we called, 'max calibrate.' We wanted to make sure we were on the same page on what we classified— this is 2A, and then this is 3B—so we had those discussions, which took a long time. We just thought that would help us to grow and evolve.

Principals Want Additional Training on Coaching Teachers

When asked what resources or training they needed for observations and conferences, administrators most frequently identified help with facilitating teacher growth and development. Ninety-four percent reported professional development on providing useful feedback and 97 percent reported coaching teachers as a high or medium training priority (**see Figure 6**).

In interviews, principals identified specific issues with providing feedback to teachers based on observations. One principal described having difficulty prioritizing areas for improvement with struggling teachers: *"There's 15 things they need to get better at, and so all 15 of them are important, where do I begin?"* Another administrator talked about struggling to find the best way to reach each individual teacher:

FIGURE 6

Most administrators report coaching and feedback as high priorities for their own training

How high a priority are the following topics for your own professional development?

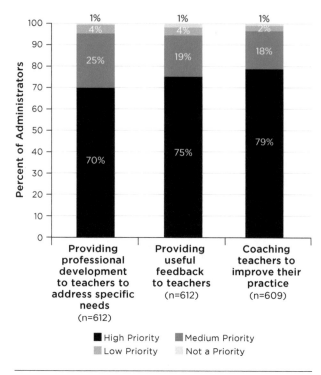

Source: Spring Administrator Survey, May 2013
Note: Percentages may not add up to 100 due to rounding.

An area I still struggle with is... when somebody's doing something wonderfully, how to be a good thought partner with making it better... Just knowing that people want different things, some people want more direct, like, "This is what you should do," and some people that turns off immediately. So it's just finding, with each individual, what is going to be the right piece to reach him or her.

A few principals described struggling with providing useful and thoughtful feedback to teachers in the time they had allotted: *"How do you do it well, and have really thoughtful conversations... I just don't know how you would get any real information and push somebody in 25 minutes?"* Another principal felt that the post-conference only allowed her time enough to report to the teacher *"what I thought she needed to work on"* and not to provide specific steps on how to improve.

Specialists also said their administrators were uneasy about conferencing with their teachers. Specialists stated some administrators were unsure of the purpose of the pre-observation conference, while other administrations told them they were feeling uneasy about leading conferences where they have to tell teachers they received lower ratings than in the past.

Training and Communication for Teachers Varied Widely

For teachers, the frequency and quality of REACH training and communication was driven largely by their school's leadership, as their school administration was by far the most common source of information about REACH (**see Figure 7**). School administrators ranged widely in what training and communication they provided their teachers and, as a result, teacher training on REACH varied widely by school. In our interview schools, we found the level of teacher training varied from no or occasional training to required weekly REACH professional development sessions. We also saw some within-school differences in REACH training,

as teachers in certain departments reported receiving occasional training and teachers in other departments reported receiving no training.

Teachers who received no training frequently reported little knowledge of REACH: *"There's a lot of questions I still have about REACH and it seems like no one really knows for sure, at least the people that I asked or talked to around my school,"* said one teacher. Another teacher was more critical of her school's administration: *"I don't feel that my school administration really put forth what exactly REACH is and how we are learning about it. I have learned more through colleagues and friends of mine who are also teachers."*

The district offered two different types of optional REACH training sessions for teachers: REACH 101, which focused on informing teachers about the details of REACH, and Teacher Talks, which provided training on the Framework and were co-sponsored by the CTU and the New Teacher Center. However, only about 400 teachers (out of the district's more than 20,000 teachers) attended these sessions. A few teachers in our interviews stated they had made the extra effort to seek

FIGURE 7

Most teachers received information about REACH through their school administration

Have you received information about REACH from any of the following sources?

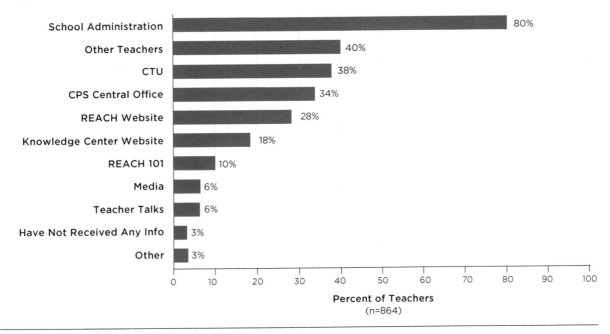

Percent of Teachers
(n=864)

Source: Winter Teacher Survey, January 2013

Note: Percentages do not add to 100 because respondents were asked to select all that apply.

The REACH website is a CPS maintained public website with information about REACH. Knowledge Center is a website with training and professional development content for CPS employees only. REACH 101 and Teacher Talks were optional sessions for teachers.

information about REACH on their own. These teachers stated they utilized the REACH website, researched the Danielson Framework on their own, or sought information from their own professional networks such as TeachPlus. Teachers did report receiving emails and resources, such as a REACH Companion Guide, at the beginning of the year; however, most teachers interviewed reported feeling reliant on their administrators for information about REACH.

Administrators reported struggling to find the time to train teachers on the Framework. Almost 80 percent of administrators surveyed cited insufficient time for training teachers on the CPS Framework as a factor in the ability of their school to effectively use the new Framework. In interviews, administrators also expressed a need for more support from the district in training their teachers.

Teachers and Administrators Need Clarity About Evaluation Score Calculation and Purpose

In interviews, teachers stated they were knowledgeable about the Framework, but reported lacking information on the other parts of REACH. Many had to be prompted or reminded that Performance Tasks and the NWEA MAP or EPAS tests were even a part of REACH. One teacher stated she was not informed that Performance Tasks were part of her evaluation until after she had already administered them:

> When I gave the REACH test in September or October, it was not until afterwards that I was informed that it was part of my evaluation. The way it was put to me was, 'Oh this is the test that's going to determine whether you're doing your job or not...' I actually felt like an idiot because I knew nothing about this.

Teachers stated they felt confused and misinformed about the weight each component would contribute to their final summative score, as well as the actual summative score calculation. Administrators also reported having only a cursory understanding of the summative calculation. Over 60 percent of administrators said

their understanding of how summative ratings are calculated was weak or moderate (**see Figure 8**).

In interviews teachers also revealed confusion over how evaluative scores might be used in personnel decisions at the school or district levels. Many teachers felt they had never received any clear communication about this. As one teacher stated in an interview:

> It left open a lot of questions as to how this might be used, or what kind of future plans the district might have for the tool. I feel that the stakes of this entire process were never clearly communicated to me.

When asked what the purpose of REACH was, answers ranged from merit pay to *"weeding out teachers"* to preparing for the Common Core. Overall, teachers expressed being uncertain about the ultimate goals of REACH.

FIGURE 8

Fewer than half of administrators had a strong understanding of how summative ratings are calculated

At this point, how would you rate your understanding of...

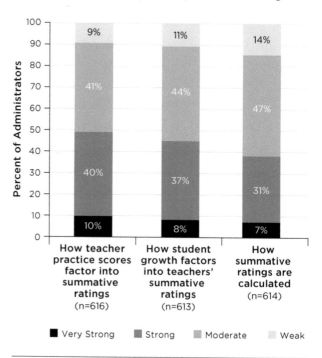

Source: Spring Administrator Survey, May 2013

Note: Percentages may not add up to 100 due to rounding.

24

CHAPTER 4

How Principals Manage Classroom Observation Workloads

Administrators were key to the school-level implementation: they were responsible for dispersing information and training their staff on REACH, in addition to conducting observations and conferences. While administrators were positive about the potential of REACH, they also expressed one common concern about the new system: the extensive time required. Sixty-six percent of administrators agreed or strongly agreed the new teacher evaluation system took too much time. When asked in an open-ended survey item to identify their biggest challenge in implementing the new system, more than 70 percent of the 588 responses concerned issues with time.

In this chapter, we focus on administrator struggles with time and balancing the requirements of this new evaluation system. We discuss first how much time administrators reported spending on the observation process. We then discuss challenges with scheduling, assigning evidence, and ratings. We end this chapter with a discussion of how principals juggled the new requirements of REACH with their other responsibilities. The quotes provided here are from principal interviews and an open-ended survey item that asked,

"What factor has been the most challenging in the ability of your school to effectively use the new Framework?"

Administrators Average Six Hours on Each Observation

In our spring survey, we asked administrators to estimate how many hours they typically spent on the three broad parts of conducting a formal observation cycle for one teacher. **Table 3** lists the activities we included in each part and gives the averages and ranges for both elementary and high school administrators. The "Total" line shows the average, minimum, and maximum reported time it took to complete one observation cycle.

On average, CPS principals report that—between the pre-conference, the observation itself, the post-conference and data entry—they spend a total of six hours on a single observation cycle for one teacher. In districts outside of Chicago utilizing a similar observation process, principals report spending the equivalent of a full day evaluating a single teacher.[36]

In the first year of REACH, administrators were directed to conduct at least four observations for each of their non-tenured teachers and at least one observation

TABLE 3

On average, administrators spend almost six hours per formal observation

Average Hours Reported for One Formal Observation for One Teacher	Elementary School Average (range)	High School Average (range)
Pre-Observation (including scheduling, preparation, and conducting the pre-conference)	1.4 (0.2-4)	1.6 (0.5-4)
Observation (including scheduling and conducting the observation, aligning evidence to the Framework, determining ratings, and entering evidence and ratings into a database)	2.8 (0.5-6)	2.8 (1-6)
Post-Observation (including scheduling, preparation, and conducting the post-conference)	1.6 (0.3-4)	1.7 (0.8-4)
Total	5.8 (1-14)	6.1 (2.3-14)

Note: Outlying values for these questions were trimmed. Some respondents may not have noticed that this question referred to time for only one teacher and one observation. About 95 percent of the responses clustered closely.

for each tenured teacher. In interviews, principals reported relying on their assistant principals to share the observation workload; thus, the observation workload was dependent on the number of administrators available and the total number of teachers in a school. In CPS, this number varies considerably. Elementary schools typically have two administrators per school (one principal and one assistant principal), while high schools typically have three administrators (one principal and two assistant principals). However, this number depends on school size; small elementary schools may have one principal and fewer than 15 teachers, while large high schools may have more than four assistant principals and more than 200 teachers. **Table 4** illustrates the staff-to-administrator ratio difference in elementary and high schools. This difference in ratio implies that high school administrators, on average, have to conduct about 50 percent more observations than elementary school administrators. The range for each category further indicates that the workload of school administrators is not equal across schools.

If we do an informal calculation using **Tables 3 and 4**, the average elementary school administrator observed approximately five non-tenured teachers four times at an average of six hours per observation. Putting these together, the average elementary administrator spent approximately 120 hours over the course of the year, which is equivalent to over two full weeks spent solely on observations, if we assume a 60-hour work week. The time estimates for high schools are greater: 168 hours or approximately three full weeks.

TABLE 4

The number of teachers per administrator varies

Average Teacher to Administrator Ratio		
	Elementary School Average (range)	High School Average (range)
Number of Non-Tenured Teachers per Administrator	4.6 (0-26)	6.9 (0-19)
Number of Tenured Teachers per Administrator	12.4 (0-35)	18.5 (3-78)

Scheduling and Managing Data Is Challenging

The timing and scheduling of classroom observations presented its own difficulties, as REACH required administrators to follow a restricted time line for conducting formal observations (see *Formal Observation Scheduling Requirements 2012-13*). Scheduled observations, however, could be cancelled at the last minute due to teacher absences or other school issues requiring administrators' immediate attention. If there was a cancellation, often all three aspects of the cycle (pre-conference, observation, post-conference) would have to be rescheduled.

While administrators were overwhelmingly positive about the Framework and the use of evidence in improving instruction-focused conversations with their teachers, the actual collection of the evidence in classrooms

Formal Observation Scheduling Requirements 2012-13

- Observations may only occur between the fifth and thirty-fifth week of school
- A pre-conference must take place at least one week prior to the observation
- Observations must last at least 45 minutes of class time and be scheduled with the teacher in advance
- A post-conference must take place within 10 days of the observation

- Observations cannot be closer together than one month for non-tenured teachers and three months for tenured teachers
- Four formal observations were required for each non-tenured teacher. One formal observation was required for each tenured teacher

and the subsequent sorting of evidence into the appropriate components in data entry presented significant time challenges. During an observation, administrators collect evidence by recording what occurs in the classroom. The evidence collected then has to be aligned by sorting it into the correct Framework component before it is entered into the system to support a rating. This process was often described as time-consuming and tedious. In an open-ended item on the survey, one administrator reported spending three hours on just reviewing, aligning and uploading evidence for each observation.

Another time-consuming aspect of evidence collection, which was identified by both administrators and specialists, was how administrators recorded their evidence. Specialists reported that the majority of administrators chose to handwrite their notes rather than type them on a laptop. In interviews, administrators also stated a preference for handwriting over typing. Having to type up handwritten notes added significant data-entry time.

Administrators Are Often Forced to Choose Between REACH and Other Responsibilities

In an interview and an open-ended item on our survey, administrators expressed frustration at wanting to spend time on REACH activities but needing to spend time on other responsibilities. They reported a desire to prioritize instructional leadership; however the reality of their job responsibilities did not give them the *"luxury of just focusing solely on instruction."* Principals have a number of non-instructional responsibilities including *"budget, HR, NCLB, state requirements, and supervising non-instructional staff such as custodians,"* as described by a principal on an open-ended survey item. In order for the new observation system to work, this principal also stated that *"CPS must take many of these non-instructional responsibilities off principals'*

plates." Overloading principals with responsibilities is becoming common in many school districts.[37]

When we interviewed administrators, we asked how they made time for REACH observations. These administrators listed trade-offs that were necessary to implement REACH as intended. For example, administrators told us that the workload of REACH caused them to spend less time talking with students or parents, coaching their teachers, and/or cultivating school climate. Others said they were participating less in grade-level or department meetings and having fewer conversations with groups of staff about schoolwide issues such as safety. Such trade-offs were also mentioned in open-ended survey responses. One administrator stated that while the new system helped identify teachers' strengths and areas of need, it left very little time to *"coach teachers on best practices."*

In interviews and on the survey, principals expressed a belief in the new process and a desire to implement the system well, but they also acknowledged that the requirements of REACH were time intensive. One administrator summarized this feeling in an open-ended survey item: *"It is extremely time-consuming and also very worthwhile...I believe this process can transform teacher and administrator collaboration if done well."*

As this chapter shows, implementation relied primarily on school administrators who had to balance new REACH responsibilities in their already full workload. As REACH moves into its second year of implementation, the number of observations each administrator must conduct increases. Non-tenured teachers will be required to have at least three formal observations and tenured teachers will be required to have at least one. In the next chapter, we pose questions for districts and policymakers to consider to sustain and improve implementation.

CHAPTER 5

Questions to Consider

As REACH and other teacher evaluation systems in districts across the nation are enacted, the questions about long-term benefits and sustainability become more complex and nuanced. Based on the findings of year one, this chapter discusses several for consideration.

The findings in this report indicate both administrators and teachers hold generally positive views toward REACH's observation process and its potential to improve instruction. Administrators feel it helps them become stronger instructional leaders; teachers welcome the opportunities for feedback, discussion, and reflection created by the process. However, teachers generally believe their evaluation relies too heavily on student growth, and many distrust the district's motives in implementing this new system. While virtually all administrators reported REACH improved their professional conversations with teachers and most reported teachers made use of their feedback, many expressed concern about the amount of time they had to spend on REACH.

The questions shaping this report were intended to provide information based on one year's implementation. However, some of the findings have implications for the initiative as it continues. For example, the distrust between teachers and the district will affect the degree of participants' ongoing support. Furthermore, at the time of this report (September 2013), teachers had not yet received their summative evaluation score; REACH in its second year will have to overcome some questions about the transparency of summative ratings, as well as their usefulness as a tool for personnel decisions. Finally, REACH will expand to include tenured teachers in the system—in observations and in student

growth. Administrators noted the time they needed to spend on the observation process in 2012-13; that will increase in 2013-14.

What can districts and stakeholders do to ensure the levels of trust necessary to successfully implement a large-scale initiative as complex as teacher evaluation?
Teacher interviews and survey responses highlight how successful implementation of REACH depended heavily on the level of trust between administrators and teachers. Such trust can help minimize the natural tension that exists when evaluation and support are provided by the same person using the same instrument. This report shows that teachers generally believed their administrator was fair and accurate—with some reservations. Those reservations were generally grounded in teachers' lack of trust that administrators would be able to set aside personal biases or would be able to provide support for self-reported weakness without harshly judging those weaknesses in the evaluation itself. In addition, we also found a notable lack of trust between teachers and the district, which, while not surprising given the events of the year, is still a concern. Many teachers mistrusted the district's motives and were suspicious about the overarching purpose of the REACH system. Yet countless studies have commented on the importance of relational trust in any kind of

educational reform or improvement.[38] As REACH continues, if there is not a level of trust and transparency across all sectors of the district, the positive sentiments toward using this system to improve practice could be replaced by contention and disengagement.

How can districts ensure adequate communication and appropriate and ongoing training across all participants in the evaluation system?
This report shows that teachers' knowledge about REACH differed widely because training and communications were largely left up to individual administrators and therefore depended on administrators' capacity to carry out this part of the initiative effectively. While information was also available online, REACH websites were not among most teachers' information sources. Good communication is too important for districts to rely on individual administrators to carry out without support and guidance from the district. Indeed, in the case of something new such as the inclusion of student growth in teacher evaluation, district support for administrators' communication with teachers is critical. At the time of this report, REACH's complex scoring rubric was not well understood by either teachers or administrators. Yet it is especially important that teachers and administrators alike understand all aspects of this new system; a lack of understanding may undermine their trust and confidence in the whole system.

In addition, ongoing training after year one is necessary to ensure administrators' ratings remain accurate and consistent with each other and over time. While teachers generally felt they were rated accurately in the first year of REACH's implementation, prior research on ratings for teacher evaluation suggests that ongoing training of evaluators and monitoring of ratings by external observers is necessary to ensure consistency and accuracy.[39] Assigning performance ratings based on observations is ultimately a matter of human judgment, which can shift over time. Without ongoing training and monitoring, familiarity bias, rater drift, and a tendency of all ratings to shift to the mean can become the norm,[40] which, like a lack of understanding and a lack of transparency, can also undermine trust and confidence in the system.

What resources or guidance can districts provide to support school leadership structures that better distribute administrators' workload?
Findings in this report indicate that successful implementation of REACH as currently designed depends primarily on the ability of school administrators to make room in their already full workloads to conduct multiple observations and hold meaningful conversations with teachers and other staff about instruction. This is obviously a daunting task. As Chapter 4 indicates, administrator workload increased substantially with the addition of REACH—and this report does not include the increased effort due to administrators' observations of other staff such as librarians and counselors who are also part of this initiative. In 2013-14 the workload will again increase dramatically; assuming the same distribution of tenured and non-tenured teachers as in 2012-13, a "typical" elementary school administrator will need to observe five non-tenured teachers and, in addition, on average, 12 tenured teachers; a total of 17 teachers must be observed multiple times. The "typical" high school administrator will need to add 19 tenured teachers to the seven non-tenured teachers that they observed in 2012-13. An informal calculation indicates these high school administrators would spend approximately 396 hours on the observation process for these 26 teachers.[41] At a conservative estimate of a 60-hour week, this would amount to six and a half weeks of work added to an already full plate. This is not an isolated case—it would be similar for about half of CPS high schools and about 25 percent of elementary schools.

Although it seems plausible that having one-on-one conversations with teachers can lead to overall improvement in student outcomes, Sebastian and Allensworth found that principal efforts to improve school climate actually led to better school-level test score increases than individual one-on-one time with teachers.[42] If the time required for REACH reduces the time available for administrators to attend to other important instructional leadership activities or if administrators need to carry the burden of all instructional and non-instructional tasks without additional support, teacher evaluation may become unsustainable and revert instead to a more elaborate form of the old checklist.

What can districts do to ensure that new teacher evaluation systems improve instruction across all schools?

This report shows that there are wide differences across schools in the size of the REACH workload for administrators, suggesting that implementation quality might vary due to this factor. Administrator workload is not the only such factor; other characteristics of leaders and of schools themselves are obviously related to the success of an initiative intended to improve instruction. Furthermore, the district has a role to play in ensuring that all administrators have access to resources such as high quality professional development for themselves and their teachers rather than relying on schools' uneven capacity to support professional growth. Indeed, in newly completed work on CPS's 2008 Excellence in Teaching Pilot, Steinberg and Sartain indicate that there were large differences across schools in the capacity of staff to capitalize on the instructional improvement focus of the pilot.[43] Schools that were already high-performing at the start of the pilot were better able to use the observation process to improve student outcomes than were schools that were struggling before the project began. This unequal capacity could be exacerbated if teachers leave struggling schools because of fears that their observation and student growth ratings—and, therefore, their chances for positive personnel actions—will be lower than they would be elsewhere. If that becomes the case, then the potentially positive effects of all of this effort may be concentrated in a subset of higher-performing schools.

REACH is a labor-intensive and complex undertaking. Leaders must find ways to build trust within schools and across the district, make the complexity more transparent, minimize or mitigate the time demands, and ensure that all schools experience the positive benefits if REACH is to fulfill its potential as a system that can differentiate levels of teacher effectiveness while simultaneously improving instruction across the whole district.

References

ACT (2013)
ACT's Educational Planning and Assessment System.
Retrieved August 8, 2013, from http://www.act.org/epas/.

Banchero, S. (2013, August 26)
Biggest Changes in a Decade Greet Students.
The Wall Street Journal. Retrieved from http://online.wsj.com/article/SB1000142412788732398060457902930353
8525902.htmll

Bryk, A.S., and Schneider, B.L. (2002)
Trust in Schools: A Core Resource for Improvement.
New York City, NY: Russell Sage Foundation.

Chicago Public Schools (2012a)
REACH Students. Retrieved August 8, 2013, from
http://www.cps.edu/reachstudents.

Chicago Public Schools (2012b)
REACH Students Teacher Practice [PowerPoint slides].
Retrieved August 8, 2013, from http://www.cps.edu/
SiteCollectionDocuments/REACH%20Students%20
Teacher%20Practice%20%282%29.pdf

Chicago Public Schools (2013)
Chicago Public Schools: Stats and facts. Retrieved
August 21, 2013, from http://www.cps.edu/about_cps/
at-a-glance/pages/stats_and_facts.aspx.

Dalton, D.R., Hitt, M.A., Certo, S.T., and Dalton, C.M. (2007)
Chapter 1: The Fundamental Agency Problem and its
Mitigation. *The Academy of Management Annals.*

Danielson, C. (2010)
Evaluations that Help Teachers Learn. *The Effective
Educator, 68*(4), 35-39.

Darling-Hammond, L. (2012)
*Creating a Comprehensive System for Evaluating and
Supporting Effective Teaching.* Stanford, CA: Stanford
Center for Opportunity Policy in Education.

Darling-Hammond, L. (2013)
*Getting Teacher Evaluation Right: What Really Matters
for Effectiveness and Improvement.* New York City, NY:
Teachers College Press.

Darling-Hammond, L., Amrein-Beardsley, A.,
Haertel, E.H., and Rothstein, J. (2011)
*Getting Teacher Evaluation Right: A Background Paper for
Policy Makers.* Washington, DC.: American Educational
Research Association and National Academy of Education.

Duke, D.L., and Stiggins, R.J. (1990)
Beyond Minimum Competence: Evaluation for
Professional Development. In J. Millman and
L. Darling-Hammond (Eds.), *The New Handbook
of Teacher Evaluation.* Newbury Park, CA: Sage.

Durlak, J.A., and DuPre, E.P. (2008)
Implementation Matters: A Review of Research on the
Influence of Implementation on Program Outcomes and
the Factors Affecting Implementation. *American Journal
of Community Psychology, 41*(3-4).

Glazerman, S., Goldhaber, D., Loeb, S., Raudenbush, S.,
Staiger, D.O., and Whitehurst, G.J. (2011)
Passing Muster: Evaluating Teacher Evaluation Systems.
Washington, DC: Brown Center on Education Policy at
Brookings.

Hallinger, P. (2005)
Instructional Leadership and the School Principal:
A Passing Fancy that Refuses to Fade Away.
Leadership and Policy in Schools, 4(3).

Hallinger, P., Bickman, L., and Davis, K. (1996)
School Context, Principal Leadership, and Student Reading
Achievement. *The Elementary School Journal, 96*(5).

Hallinger, P., and Heck, R.H. (1998)
Exploring the Principal's Contribution to School
Effectiveness: 1980-1995. *School Effectiveness and
School Improvement, 9*(2).

Halverson, R., Grigg, J., Prichett, R., and Thomas, C. (2007)
The New Instructional Leadership: Creating Data-Driven
Instructional Systems in School. *Journal of School
Leadership, 17.*

Hansen, M. (2013)
*Anticipating Innovation in Teacher Evaluation Systems:
Lessons for Researchers and Policymakers.* Washington,
DC: American Enterprise Institute.

Hanushek, E.A., and Rivkin, S.G. (2010)
Generalizations about Using Value-Added Measures of
Teacher Quality. *American Economic Review, 100*(2), 4.

Healey, K. (2013)
Teachers, Networks, and Social Capital. Ann Arbor, MI:
UMI Dissertation Publishing.

Heitin, L. (2012)
Chicago Strike Puts Spotlight on Teacher-Evaluation Reform, *Education Week.*

Ho, A.D., and Kane, T.J. (2013)
The Reliability of Classroom Research by School Personnel. Seattle, WA: Bill & Melinda Gates Foundation.

Humphrey, D.C., Koppich, J.E., Bland, J.A., and Bosetti, K.R. (2011)
Getting Serious about Teacher Support and Evaluation. Menlo Park, CA: SRI International.

Joe, J.N., Tocci, C.N., Holtzman, S.L., and Williams, J.C. (2013)
Foundations of Observation: Considerations for Developing a Classroom Observation System that Helps Districts Achieve Consistent and Accurate Scores. Seattle, WA: Bill & Melinda Gates Foundation.

Kane, T.J., and Staiger, D.O. (2012)
Gathering Feedback for Teaching: Combining High-Quality Observations with Student Surveys and Achievement Gains. Seattle, WA: Bill & Melinda Gates Foundation.

Louis, K.S., Dretzke, B., and Wahlstrom, K. (2010)
How Does Leadership Affect Student Achievement? Results from a National U.S. Survey. *School Effectiveness and School Improvement, 21*(3).

Mead, S., Rotherham, A., and Brown, R. (2012)
The Hangover: Thinking about the Unintended Consequences of the Nation's Teacher Evaluation Binge. Washington, DC: American Enterprise Institute.

Nye, B., Konsantopoulos, S., and Hedges, L.V. (2004)
How Large Are Teacher Effects? *Educational Evaluation and Policy Analysis, 26*(3), 237-257.

Performance Evaluation Reform Act (2010)
Law of Illinois, 2010. Illinois Public Act 096-0861.

Sartain, L., Stoelinga, S.R., and Brown, E.R. (2011)
Rethinking Teacher Evaluation in Chicago. Chicago, IL: Consortium on Chicago School Research.

Sebastian, J., and Allensworth, E. (2012)
The Influence of Principal Leadership on Classroom Instruction and Student Learning: A Study of Mediated Pathways to Learning. *Educational Administration Quarterly, 48*(4).

Stein, M.K., and D'Amico, L. (2000)
How Subjects Matter in School Leadership. Paper presented at the American Educational Research Association, New Orleans, LA.

Stein, M.K., and Nelson, B.S. (2003)
Leadership Content Knowledge. *Educational Evaluation and Policy Analysis, 25*(4).

Steinberg, M.P., and Sartain, L. (Forthcoming)
Does Teacher Evaluation Improve School Performance? *Education Finance and Policy.*

Taylor, E.S., and Tyler, J.H. (2012)
The Effect of Evaluation on Teacher Performance. *The American Economic Review, 102*(7), 3628-3651.

The Danielson Group (2011)
The Framework for Teaching. Retrieved August 16, 2013, from http://www.danielsongroup.org/article.aspx?page=frameworkforteaching.

TNTP (2010)
Teacher Evaluation 2.0. New York City, NY: TNTP.

U.S. Department of Education (2009)
Race to the Top Executive Summary. Washington, DC

Weisberg, D., Sexton, S., Mulhern, J., and Keeling, D. (2009)
The Widget Effect: Our National Failure to Acknowledge and Act on Differences in Teacher Effectiveness. New York City, NY: TNTP.

White, B.R., Cowhy, J., Stevens, W.D., and Sporte, S.E. (2012)
Designing and Implementing the Next Generation of Teacher Evaluation Systems: Lessons Learned from Case Studies in Five Illinois Districts. Chicago, IL: Consortium on Chicago School Research.

Wright, S.P., Horn, S.P., and Sanders, W.L. (1997)
Teacher and Classroom Context Effects on Student Achievement: Implications for Teacher Evaluation. *Journal of Personnel Evaluation in Education, 11,* 57-67.

34

Appendix A
Chicago Public Schools Evaluation Checklist

CLASSROOM TEACHER VISITATION (Required)

Teacher's Name:_____ Room _____ Date _____

School_____ Subject/Grade_____

(Place a (√) or brief comment in the appropriate column.)

I Instruction	Strength	Weakness	Does Not Apply
A. Provides written lesson plans and preparation in accordance with the objectives of the instructional program.			
B. Establishes positive learning expectation standards for all students.			
C. Periodically evaluates pupils' progress and keeps up-to-date records of pupils' achievements.			
D. Applies contemporary principles of learning theory and teaching methodology.			
E. Draws from the range of instruction materials available in the school.			
F. Exhibits willingness to participate in the development and implementation of new ideas and teaching techniques.			
G. Provides bulletin board and interest areas reflective of current student work.			
H. Exhibits and applies knowledge of the curriculum content related to subject area and instructional level.			
I. Shows evidence of student performance and progress.			

II School Environment	Strength	Weakness	Does Not Apply
A. Establishes and maintains reasonable rules of conduct within the classroom consistent with the provisions of the Student Code of Conduct.			
B. Maintains attendance books, lesson plan, seating chart(s) and grade book accurately.			
C. Uses recommendations and suggestions from conference and special education staffings.			
D. Encourages student growth in self discipline and positive self-concept.			
E. Makes students aware of the teacher's objectives and expectations.			
F. Practices fairness in teacher-pupil relationships.			
G. Exhibits an understanding and respect for students as individuals.			

III Professional and Personal Standards	Strength	Weakness	Does Not Apply
A. Presents an appearance that does not adversely affect the students' ability to learn.			
B. Demonstrates proper diction and grammatical usage when addressing students.			
C. Uses sound and professional judgment.			

IV Local School Unit Criteria	Strength	Weakness	Does Not Apply
A.			
B.			
C.			

Appendix B
The CPS Framework for Teaching (abbreviated version)

The CPS Framework for Teaching

Adapted from the Danielson Framework for Teaching and Approved by Charlotte Danielson

Domain 1: Planning and Preparation

a. Demonstrating Knowledge of Content and Pedagogy
Knowledge of Content Standards Within and Across Grade Levels
Knowledge of Disciplinary Literacy
Knowledge of Prerequisite Relationships
Knowledge of Content-Related Pedagogy

b. Demonstrating Knowledge of Students
Knowledge of Child and Adolescent Development
Knowledge of the Learning Process
Knowledge of Students' Skills, Knowledge, and Language Proficiency
Knowledge of Students' Interests and Cultural Heritage
Knowledge of Students' Special Needs and Appropriate
   Accommodations/Modifications

c. Selecting Instructional Outcomes
Sequence and Alignment
Clarity
Balance

d. Designing Coherent Instruction
Unit/Lesson Design that Incorporates Knowledge of Students and
   Student Needs
Unit/Lesson Alignment of Standards-Based Objectives, Assessments,
   and Learning Tasks
Use of a Variety of Complex Texts, Materials and Resources, including
   Technology
Instructional Groups
Access for Diverse Learners

e. Designing Student Assessment
Congruence with Standards-Based Learning Objectives
Levels of Performance and Standards
Design of Formative Assessments
Use for Planning

Domain 2: The Classroom Environment

a. Creating an Environment of Respect and Rapport
Teacher Interaction with Students, including both Words and Actions
Student Interactions with One Another, including both Words and
   Actions

b. Establishing a Culture for Learning
Importance of Learning
Expectations for Learning and Achievement
Student Ownership of Learning

c. Managing Classroom Procedures
Management of Instructional Groups
Management of Transitions
Management of Materials and Supplies
Performance of Non-Instructional Duties
Direction of Volunteers and Paraprofessionals

d. Managing Student Behavior
Expectations and Norms
Monitoring of Student Behavior
Fostering Positive Student Behavior
Response to Student Behavior

Domain 4: Professional Responsibilities

a. Reflecting on Teaching and Learning
Effectiveness
Use in Future Teaching

b. Maintaining Accurate Records
Student Completion of Assignments
Student Progress in Learning
Non-Instructional Records

c. Communicating with Families
Information and Updates about Grade Level Expectations and Student
   Progress
Engagement of Families and Guardians as Partners in the Instructional
   Program
Response to Families
Cultural Appropriateness

d. Growing and Developing Professionally
Enhancement of Content Knowledge and Pedagogical Skill
Collaboration and Professional Inquiry to Advance Student Learning
Participation in School Leadership Team and/or Teacher Teams
Incorporation of Feedback

e. Demonstrating Professionalism
Integrity and Ethical Conduct
Commitment to College and Career Readiness
Advocacy
Decision-Making
Compliance with School and District Regulations

Domain 3: Instruction

a. Communicating with Students
Standards-Based Learning Objectives
Directions for Activities
Content Delivery and Clarity
Use of Oral and Written Language

b. Using Questioning and Discussion Techniques
Use of Low- and High-Level Questioning
Discussion Techniques
Student Participation and Explanation of Thinking

c. Engaging Students in Learning
Standards-Based Objectives and Task Complexity
Access to Suitable and Engaging Texts
Structure, Pacing and Grouping

d. Using Assessment in Instruction
Assessment Performance Levels
Monitoring of Student Learning with Checks for Understanding
Student Self-Assessment and Monitoring of Progress

e. Demonstrating Flexibility and Responsiveness
Lesson Adjustment
Response to Student Needs
Persistence
Intervention and Enrichment

2012

36

Endnotes

Executive Summary

1 Sartain, Stoelinga, and Brown (2011).

2 Weisberg, Sexton, Mulhern, and Keeling (2009).

3 Sartain, Stoelinga, and Brown (2011).

Introduction

4 See Appendix A for CPS's Checklist System.

5 Banchero (2013); Heitin (2012).

6 Hansen (2013).

7 Hanushek and Rivkin (2010); Nye, Konstantopoulos, and Hedges (2004); Wright, Horn and Sanders (1997).

8 US Department of Education (2009).

9 Although not included in this report, PERA also includes changes to how school leaders are evaluated.

10 For more information on the Charlotte Danielson Framework for Teaching, see http://www.danielson-group.org/article.aspx?page=frameworkforteaching.

11 Steinberg and Sartain (Forthcoming); Taylor and Tyler (2012).

12 For examples, see Kane and Staiger (2012); Glazerman, et al. (2011).

13 Darling-Hammond (2012); Humphrey, Koppich, Bland, and Bosetti (2011).

14 Duke and Stiggins (1990).

15 Healey (2013).

16 Healey (2013).

17 Mead, Rotherham, and Brown (2012); Ho and Kane (2013); Darling-Hammond, Amrein-Beardsley, Haertel, and Rothstein (2011).

18 Sartain, Stoelinga, and Brown (2011).

19 See Darling-Hammond, Amrein-Beardsley, Haertel, and Rothstein (2011) for a review of the literature critiquing value-added models.

20 TNTP (2010).

21 Durlak and DuPre (2008).

22 Dalton, Hitt, Certo, and Dalton (2007).

23 Hallinger (2005); Hallinger, Bickman, and Davis (1996); Hallinger and Heck (1998); Halverson, Grigg, Prichett, and Thomas (2007); Louis, Dretzke, and Wahlstrom (2010); Stein and D'Amico (2000); Stein and Nelson (2003).

24 Sartain, Stoelinga, and Brown (2011); White, Cowhy, Stevens, and Sporte (2012).

Chapter 1

25 Kane and Staiger (2012); Ho and Kane (2013).

26 Darling-Hammond, Amrein-Beardsley, Haertel, and Rothstein (2011).

Chapter 2

27 At the time our data were collected, teachers had only administered the beginning-of-year assessments.

28 The EPAS assessments were administered without stakes for teachers' evaluation during the first year of REACH.

29 The survey also included an open-ended question about what teachers found most promising about REACH. Just 3 percent of the 532 teachers who responded to this question indicated that they found the student growth component to be the most promising aspect of REACH.

30 For 2013-14, CPS has reduced the number of required assessments.

31 Under PERA's requirements districts must consider how student characteristics like special education placement will be used in calculating student growth; CPS has not publicly provided detail on any possible adjustment in student growth measures for special education students.

32 Chicago Public Schools (2012a).

33 Some schools also administer a middle-of-year NWEA MAP assessment, but students' scores on the middle-of-year assessment are not used in the calculation of student growth. For 2013-14, the value-added calculation will be based on changes in students' scores from the spring of one year to the spring of the following year.

34 It should be noted that the EPAS assessments are not designed for this purpose. They are intended to gauge student readiness for college and career. See ACT (2013) for more information.

Chapter 3

35 This number includes administrators new to the system who had not yet had time to complete the certification process.

Chapter 4

36 Darling-Hammond (2013).

37 Darling-Hammond (2013).

Chapter 5

38 For example, see Bryk and Schneider (2002).

39 Ho and Kane (2013); Joe, J.N., Tocci, C.N., Holtzman, S.L., and Williams, J.C. (2013); Danielson (2010).

40 Joe, et al. (2013).

41 Informal calculation is based on administrators' reports of spending 6 hours per formal observation, an estimate of 3 hours per informal observation, and the requirement that non-tenured teachers have three formal plus one informal observation and tenured teachers have one of each type in 2013-14. Teacher to administrator ratios calculated from fall 2012 personnel records.

42 Sebastian and Allensworth (2012).

43 Steinberg and Sartain (Forthcoming).

Sidebars

A Non-tenured teachers, who represented 30 percent of the workforce in fall 2012, were oversampled. We used survey weights to adjust for this oversampling in all analyses of this survey throughout this report.

B Sartain, Stoelinga, and Brown (2011).

C Steinberg and Sartain (Forthcoming).

D Performance Evaluation Reform Act (2010).

E The PERA legislation gave CPS, by far the largest district in Illinois, the option to adopt a Type I state assessment as its sole measure of student growth. If CPS determined the state assessment to be inappropriate for measuring student growth, it then must also use (1) a Type I or Type II and (2) a Type III assessment.

ABOUT THE AUTHORS

SUSAN E. SPORTE is Director for Research Operations at UChicago CCSR. Her current research focuses on teacher preparation and measuring effective teaching. Prior to joining UChicago CCSR, she worked as a community college math instructor and as a college administrator. Sporte holds a BS from Michigan State University, an MA from the University of Illinois at Springfield, and an EdM and EdD from the Harvard Graduate School of Education.

W. DAVID STEVENS is Director for Research Engagement at the UChicago CCSR. Stevens' responsibilities include developing trainings and workshops to help practitioners, policymakers, and school districts understand UChicago CCSR's research findings and use them in their daily practice. Stevens also leads national engagement activities, working with individuals and organizations interested in reproducing UChicago CCSR's model of education research. Stevens' research interests include high school reform, teacher development, and student engagement. Stevens received his PhD in sociology from Northwestern University.

KALEEN HEALEY is a Senior Research Analyst at UChicago CCSR. She joined UChicago CCSR after earning her PhD in human development and social policy from Northwestern University. She previously directed a college and career readiness program in Chicago and taught in the Saint Louis Public Schools through Teach for America. She holds a BFA from the University of Notre Dame and an MA from Loyola University Chicago.

JENNIE JIANG is a Research Analyst at UChicago CCSR. She previously worked as a researcher at Chapin Hall and as a teacher, both in Chicago Public Schools and in Shenzen, China. She earned an MPP in public policy at the Harris School of Public Policy at the University of Chicago and an MS in education at Northwestern University.

HOLLY HART is a Senior Research Analyst at UChicago CCSR. She is currently working on an evaluation of the Urban Teacher Education Program (UChicago UTEP) and a study of the effectiveness of school leadership practices in addition to her work on teacher evaluation. Dr. Hart has conducted quantitative and qualitative studies of school leaders graduating from three different preparation programs and how these leaders rely on their National Board Certified teachers. She received her PhD in human development and social policy from Northwestern University.

40

This report reflects the interpretation of the authors. Although UChicago CCSR's Steering Committee provided technical advice, no formal endorsement by these individuals, organizations, or the full Consortium should be assumed.

UCHICAGOCCSR

CONSORTIUM ON CHICAGO SCHOOL RESEARCH

Directors

ELAINE M. ALLENSWORTH
Lewis-Sebring Director
Consortium on Chicago
School Research

JENNY NAGAOKA
Deputy Director
Consortium on Chicago
School Research

MELISSA RODERICK
*Hermon Dunlap Smith
Professor*
School of Social Service
Administration
University of Chicago

PENNY BENDER SEBRING
Founding Director
Consortium on Chicago
School Research

Steering Committee

LILA LEFF
Co-Chair
Umoja Student Development
Corporation

KATHLEEN ST. LOUIS
Co-Chair
Spark, Chicago

Ex-Officio Members

TIMOTHY KNOWLES
Urban Education Institute

Institutional Members

JOHN R. BARKER
Chicago Public Schools

CLARICE BERRY
Chicago Principals and
Administrators Association

AARTI DHUPELIA
Chicago Public Schools

CHRISTOPHER KOCH
Illinois State Board of
Education

KAREN G.J. LEWIS
Chicago Teachers Union

SHERRY J. ULERY
Chicago Public Schools

Individual Members

VERONICA ANDERSON
Communications Consultant

JOANNA BROWN
Logan Square Neighborhood
Association

ANDREW BROY
Illinois Network of
Charter Schools

RAQUEL FARMER-HINTON
University of Wisconsin,
Milwaukee

REYNA HERNANDEZ
Illinois State Board of
Education

CHRIS JONES
Stephen T. Mather
High School

DENNIS LACEWELL
Urban Prep Charter Academy
for Young Men

**RUANDA GARTH
MCCULLOUGH**
Loyola University

LUISIANA MELÉNDEZ
Erikson Institute

LISA SCRUGGS
Jenner and Block

LUIS R. SORIA
Chicago Public Schools

BRIAN SPITTLE
DePaul University

MATTHEW STAGNER
Chicago Human Services
Research

AMY TREADWELL
Chicago New Teacher Center

ARIE J. VAN DER PLOEG
American Institutes for
Research

KIM ZALENT
Business and Professional
People for the Public Interest